Plants and Humans

Claire Llewellyn

FRANKLIN WATTS

First published in 2006 by
Franklin Watts
338 Euston Road
London NW1 3BH

Franklin Watts Australia
Hachette Children's Books
Level 17/207 Kent Street
Sydney NSW 2000

Editor: Jennifer Schofield
Art director: Jonathan Hair
Consultant: Caroline Boisset
Design: Susi Martin
Picture researcher: Diana Morris
Artwork: Ian Thompson
Photography: Ray Moller, unless otherwise acknowledged

Acknowledgements:
Tevje Bendiksby/Camera Press: 27r. BSIP Chassenet/SPL: 19. Nigel Cattlin/FLPA: 25t.
David R. Frazier/Image Works/Topfto: 23. Pascal Goetgheluck/SPL: 20. Historical Picture
Archive/Corbis: 25b. Holt Studios/FLPA: 6, 10b, 11, 13tl, 14, 15, 16, 21b, 22, 24cl, 26,
29c, 29cr, 29bl. J. Jaemsen/zefa/Corbis: 3, 29cl. Caroline Penn/Corbis: 12. Alexis Rosenfeld/
SPL: 27bl. Tony Savino/Image Works/Topfoto: 17t. Topfoto: front cover, 7t.

The publisher would like to thank Biopac
for supplying the corn starch bag on page 7

A CIP catalogue record for this book
is available from the British Library.

ISBN-10: 0 7496 6512 2
ISBN-13: 978 0 7496 6512 8
Dewey Classification: 581'6
Printed in China

Contents

Using plants

People have always made use of plants. Many thousands of years ago, our ancestors gathered plants for food and fuel. Today, we depend on plants for many other things, too – from jeans and juice to socks and soap.

What makes plants useful?

Every species of plant has its own special properties. These could be something to do with the plant's structure or its taste, or a substance it produces. Any part of the plant may be useful: the roots, stems, sap, buds, leaves, flowers, fruits or seeds. Some plants have just one useful part. The rubber plant is grown for its milky sap and the coffee plant for its berries. Other plants have several useful parts. For example, the trunk and leaves of the coconut palm can be used as building materials and the fruit – coconuts – provide not only food and drink, but also fibres for making rope and matting, and oils for soaps and fuel.

Try this!

Have a look in a garden or park and make a list of the different plants you can see. Think about the special properties of each plant. Why do you think each plant has been planted?

The sticky sap that is collected from rubber trees is known as latex. As it dries, the latex becomes stretchy and can be used to make rubber.

A woman from Sri Lanka plaits the leaves of a coconut palm. These will be used to make walls and roofs.

The diversity of plants

Our ancestors made use of local plants. With technological advances, such as air travel, we can now use plants from all over the world. Scientists estimate that there are over 400,000 different plant species on Earth – many of which are still unknown. If each plant has its own special properties, the potential of plants is huge! This book looks at plants and examines the role that some of them play in our everyday lives.

Get this!

Scientists are always finding new ways of using plants. Corn starch from the maize plant can now be used to make biodegradable carrier bags, which – unlike plastic bags – safely rot away.

Plants feed us

Plants provide us with many different foods in a huge variety of shapes, colours, textures, smells and tastes. Plants are also rich in many nutrients that are good for our bodies.

Plants in our diet

Unlike humans, plants make their own food (see page 18) and so are the start of the food chain. They are important for our diet and provide us with a range of nutrients. Wheat, maize, rice and other grains are packed with energy-rich carbohydrates. Pulses, the seeds of the pea and bean family, contain body-building proteins. Fruits and vegetables provide minerals and vitamins, which help us to stay healthy. Other plants add interest to our diet. For example, herbs and spices add wonderful flavours to food. Favourite treats such as sugar, chocolate, cola and tea are also made from plants.

Juicy fruits, crunchy nuts, vegetables and herbs... plants add variety and goodness to our diet. It is hard to imagine life without them.

Try this!

For one day, keep a note of everything you eat and drink. How much of it was made from plants? Do you know where they were grown?

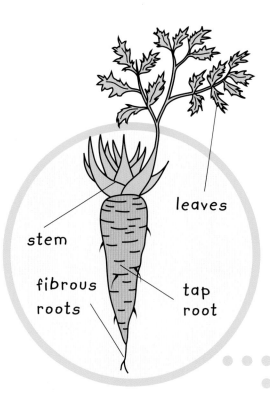

stem

leaves

fibrous roots

tap root

The carrot plant grows roots, stems and leaves. We eat only the sweet, swollen tap root and discard the rest.

Processing the food

We eat only the best and tastiest parts of a plant. It may be the root, stem, leaves, flower, fruits or seeds. Many of these foods can be eaten fresh but they may also be dried, canned, frozen or turned into juice. Other foods may need further processing – for example, wheat grains are milled to produce flour. Some plant foods, such as lettuce, can be eaten raw. Others, such as potatoes and rice, are only eaten cooked.

Get this!

Even some sea plants can be eaten. Sushi is a popular Japanese rice dish made with fish and vegetables. Often, it is wrapped in black seaweed.

Home or away?

Many of the fruits and vegetables we buy in shops are grown locally in a particular season of the year. However, a lot of foods – for example strawberries and peas – are also grown in warmer places, and can be supplied to us all year round. Air-freighting food over thousands of kilometres uses vast amounts of energy, which increases air pollution and adds to global warming. It is better to buy local produce whenever we can.

Plants on the farm

The first farmers began to cultivate plants thousands of years ago. Today, agriculture is a huge business, using mighty machines and modern methods to feed a global population of over six billion.

Breeding plants

About 10,000 years ago, people began to collect seeds from plants and sow them in the ground. This was the beginning of agriculture. With so many different plants available, people began to experiment, taking seeds from species that grew easily or provided better yields. In this way, people 'bred' domestic plant varieties. Plant breeding continues today with scientists developing new varieties that may be tastier, juicier, more nutritious or abundant, or more resistant to the harmful effects of pests, disease or cold.

Breeding has produced different types of tomato – from the huge beefsteak, to the tiny cherry and plum varieties.

Polytunnels provide extra warmth. Farmers use them to extend the growing season for tender crops.

Farming methods

In many parts of the world, farming is highly mechanised so that large quantities of crops can be grown by a small workforce. Chemical fertilisers are added to the soil to provide plants with extra nutrients, such as nitrogen and potassium. Chemicals are also used to kill weeds and pests. In more temperate regions, some crops, such as tomatoes, are grown in glasshouses or polytunnels, which provide extra light and warmth. The crops are grown in artificial 'soil' and are drip-fed water and nutrients.

Organic farmers do not use chemicals on their land, instead they add manure to the soil to fertilise it and keep it healthy.

What's this?

This plant was once a kind of wild grass. Today it is one of the world's most important food crops, and its grains are used to make flour. The flour is used to make pasta and bread.

Organic farming

In recent years, people have questioned modern farming methods. They argue that agricultural chemicals poison wildlife, pollute rivers and streams, and are harmful to our health. They want sustainable farming in which farmers think about future effects on the environment and work with nature, rather than against it. Organic farming is also growing in importance. It uses natural fertilisers such as manure, compost or seaweed. Organic farming also uses natural methods of pest control, such as encouraging pest-eating insects or so-called 'companion' planting – for example, planting onions with carrots to deter carrot-fly.

Plants clothe us

Plant fibres can be spun and woven and turned into comfortable, hard-wearing cotton and other kinds of cloth. Other plant materials are also used to make dyes, shoes and hats.

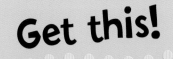

Get this!

Sombreros, panamas and many other hats are made from woven grass stalks – otherwise known as straw.

Working with fibres

If you pull a plant apart, you will see that it is made of stringy fibres. In some plants the fibres are strong, flexible and reasonably soft. For thousands of years, people have knotted or plaited the fibres to make simple clothes, or they have processed them to make cloth. The ancient crafts of spinning and weaving transformed plant fibres into hard-wearing textiles. Since the early 1800s, this work has been done by machines.

These women from Sierra Leone in West Africa are dyeing cotton cloth. They will then make it into clothes.

Inside a cotton plant's seed cases are masses of fluffy seeds. The seeds are used to make fabric.

Try this!

Use plants to dye a white cotton T-shirt. To make the dye, cut up the skins of 6 large onions for yellow dye, 500g of beetroot for red dye, or 250g of spinach for green dye. Soak whichever vegetables you are using overnight in enough water to cover the T-shirt. Then, ask an adult to help you to simmer the vegetables for an hour. Remove them, put the T-shirt in the pot and simmer for 30 minutes. Leave the T-shirt to soak for several hours. Use gloves to remove the shirt, then rinse and dry it.

From seeds and stems

Fibres are taken from many plant species, and from different parts of the plant. Cotton is made from the seeds of the cotton plant. These are covered in strong, silky hairs, designed to spread the seeds on the wind. These silky hairs are collected and spun into yarn. Linen, another important cloth, is made from the stems of a plant called flax. Soaking and drying the smooth, straight flax stems allows the fibres to be separated. They can then be combed, twisted and spun into yarn, then woven into cloth.

Plants on the feet

Plant materials are also used to make shoes. As we walk, our feet hit the hard ground and need protection from the impact. Shoe soles made from wood, cork and rubber are springy and they absorb the shock. Rubber is used to make wellington boots because it is waterproof and keeps feet dry.

Plants house us

We use plants to build and furnish our homes. Wood, bamboo, rattan, wicker, reeds, cork and coir are just some of the hard-wearing, attractive materials we use to live in, walk on and sit on.

Made of wood

Wood is an important construction material. It is strong and long-lasting and it can be used as the supportive framework for a building and for window frames, doors and floors. Most of the timber used for building comes from conifers such as pine, spruce and fir.

Wood is used to build houses in places with cold winters because it is a good insulator and helps to lock in the heat.

Bamboo houses

In tropical regions, millions of people live in homes made of bamboo. Bamboo is a kind of grass which grows strong, but lightweight, tube-shaped stems. These are easily harvested and are used to make pillars, walls, window frames, rafters, ceilings and roofs. A bamboo home is cool and airy, and it is particularly safe in earthquake zones because it is so light.

What's this?

This tree has a light, springy, waterproof bark. It is used to make floor tiles, shoes and stoppers for wine bottles.

Inside the home

We use other plant materials to furnish our homes. Plant stems such as wicker (from the willow tree), rattan (from tropical climbing plants), and rushes (from reedbeds) can all be woven to create light, sturdy furniture and comfortable seats. Cork tiles are suitable for flooring because they are warm, hard-wearing and an excellent soundproofer. Coir, the coarse fibre from coconut shells, is also found on floors – in the doormats we use to wipe our feet.

The cork oak grows around the Mediterranean Sea. The tree grows a thick layer of cork under its bark, which can be removed in sheets.

Get this!

A pine tree needs at least 20 years to reach a suitable size for building. Bamboo can be harvested after just one year.

The wonders of wood

What would we do without wood? It floats, burns, insulates sound and heat and has many other useful properties. These, along with its availability, make wood one of the world's most important materials.

Wood floats

Most kinds of wood will float in water. That is why wood has always been used to build sailing boats, canoes and other kinds of craft. Boats are a vital form of transport, both for fishing and transporting people and goods. They are used on rivers and seas all over the world.

In China, as in every part of the world, people use wood to build fishing boats and other sailing craft.

What's this?

This broad-leaved tree can live for 1,000 years. Its fruit is the acorn and its wood is strong and slow to rot. It has been used to build ships, churches, houses and furniture.

Wood burns

People have always depended on wood to make fires for cooking their food and to keep them warm. This is because wood burns easily and gives out plenty of heat. Unlike other fuels, such as coal, oil or gas, wood can be easily gathered. It is still the most important fuel for millions of people.

Wood makes music

Many musical instruments are made of wood. This is because wood is a good insulator – in other words, it forms a barrier to sound vibrations. The vibrations made by instruments such as recorders, guitars or violins cannot easily pass through the wooden case. Instead, they roll around inside, making a richer, louder sound.

Wood makes paper

Paper is such a common material that it is easy to forget that it is made from plants. Paper is made from chopped wood fibres, which are mixed with water to make a soggy mass called wood pulp. As the pulp is flattened and dried, it forms paper, which can then be treated in various ways to make tissue, cardboard, stationery and other paper goods.

This musician is playing an acoustic guitar made of wood. As she plucks the strings, vibrations enter the sound box, creating musical sounds.

Try this!

Collect several different kinds of paper and tear them. Now take a magnifying glass and look along the torn edge. Can you see any fibres?

Plants give us oxygen

Every breath we take depends on plants. This is because plants produce oxygen, the gas we and other animals need to survive. Plants do this through an important process known as photosynthesis.

What is photosynthesis?

Plants are living things and need food to survive. Unlike animals, which have to hunt for food, plants can make food for themselves. They do this by a process called photosynthesis, which takes place inside their leaves.

The leaves use energy from sunlight, water and a gas from the air called carbon dioxide to make sugary and starchy sustances called carbohydrates. As this process takes place, each leaf produces a precious waste product: a tiny puff of oxygen.

PHOTOSYNTHESIS

Oxygen and some water is given off into the air.

Leaves soak up sunlight. Carbon dioxide enters the leaves from the air.

Water is taken in through the roots.

Water moves up the stem to the leaves.

Try this!

Use a clear glass to scoop up some pondweed. Allow the pondweed to settle so that it floats to the top of the glass and the water clears. Leave the glass in a sunny place, and after a few hours you will be able to see bubbles of oxygen made by the pondweed.

A balance of gases

The air we breathe is made up of a mixture of gases, including oxygen and carbon dioxide. Plants play an important role in balancing these gases. Every day they remove vast amounts of carbon dioxide from the air and replace it with oxygen. Animals inhale the oxygen and exhale carbon dioxide. Without plants, our supply of oxygen would soon run out.

When we breathe in, we take in oxygen from the air. This oxygen is produced by plants. We cannot live without it.

Global warming

In recent years, cars, factories and power stations have produced a build-up of carbon dioxide – the waste gas produced by burning oil and other fossil fuels. Carbon dioxide traps the Sun's heat, and is making our planet warmer. This contributes to what is known as global warming. Global warming causes ice caps to melt and sea levels to rise. It may also cause severe weather, such as droughts and storms. Plants can help to slow down global warming because they absorb carbon dioxide and replace it with oxygen.

Get this!

An average-sized lawn produces enough oxygen in a week for one person's daily demand.

Plants and the body

We use all kinds of plants to care for our bodies. Some contain chemicals that relieve pain or fight germs and disease. Others contain oils that are good for our skin and keep us smelling sweet.

Healing power

Have you ever been stung by stinging nettles and used a dock leaf to ease the sting? This is an example of a plant remedy. Plants are living chemical factories. They have evolved powerful substances, some of which can be used to help us. About 100 years ago, the leaves and bark of the willow tree were used to develop the drug aspirin, an important pain-killer.

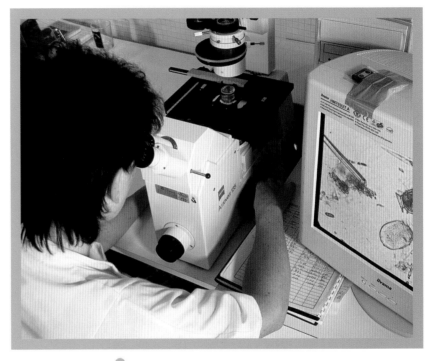

By studying the substances in plants, scientists have produced medicines to fight serious diseases such as malaria.

What's this?

This low woody plant has purple-blue spiky flowers. Its oils are sweet-smelling and are used to make soaps and perfumes.

Keeping us clean

People have used plants to clean themselves for thousands of years. The ancient Egyptians, Greeks and Romans all used plant oils to clean and care for their skin. Some of today's soaps, shampoos and hair conditioners contain oils from coconuts, almonds, avocados and many other plants.

Get this!

About 500 years ago, sweet-smelling herbs such as rosemary and sage were scattered on the floor to mask bad smells and deter fleas and lice.

Try this!

Mint is good for the stomach. Next time you have a stomach ache, wash a stem or two of mint and put it in a mug. Fill the mug with boiling water, leave to stand for 10 minutes, then slowly sip the drink.

Plant aromas

Many plants have wonderful aromas, and their oils can be used to make perfumes. Many oils, such as jasmine, honeysuckle, lavender and rose, are made from the flower of the plant. Some, such as rosemary, are made from the leaves, while others, such as vanilla and sandalwood, are made from seed pods or fragrant wood.

The lavender plant is grown commercially. Its aromatic oils are used in perfumes, soap, bath oil and creams.

Dangerous plants

Many plants contain powerful chemicals. Sometimes these chemicals can be useful but, without proper care, they can be very dangerous. We must always be careful around plants and treat them with respect.

A dangerous defence

Many plants defend themselves by producing substances that are so nasty that animals will avoid them. If we accidentally eat these plants – some of which grow in parks and gardens – they can harm us. Some plants cause allergies or irritate the skin, but others can kill. In some species, such as the yew tree, every part of the plant is dangerous. In others, there is only one poisonous part – for example, the berries of the holly tree, the seeds of the violet, and the leaves of the rhubarb plant.

Warning!

Never eat any part of a plant unless an adult tells you it is safe.

Get this!

Deadly nightshade is a poisonous plant. In ancient Greece, women dropped its juices into their eyes because it made their pupils larger and gave them a 'wide-eyed' look.

Many people grow rhubarb in their gardens. The juicy pink stalks are good to eat, but the leaves are poisonous.

Fishing with poison

Native peoples in Guyana, Brazil and other parts of the world use poisonous plants to help them to catch fish. First they pound and mash the plants, then they put them into ponds and slow-moving streams. The chemicals from the plants stun nearby fish, which float to the surface and can be easily caught. The effect of the poison is short-lived, and any fish that is not captured recovers soon afterwards.

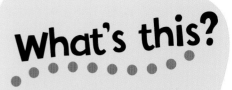

Harmful drugs

Some plants can be used to make harmful drugs. For example, the dried leaves of the tobacco plant, which are used to make cigarettes, contain a dangerous substance called nicotine. Smoking cigarettes harms the body, causing many kinds of illness and disease. Yet the nicotine in them creates an addiction that makes it very hard to stop. Every year, thousands of people die as a result of smoking.

Tobacco leaves are hung out to dry before being processed into cigarettes. Smoking tobacco is very harmful to the body.

Plants that inspire

Plants have evolved special features to solve the problems of survival. Some of them have inspired engineers and inventors to create new, useful materials and tools.

Velcro can be used to fasten shoes. Its invention was inspired by the tiny hooks that are found on burdock seeds.

A new fastening

The burdock plant was the inspiration for the invention of Velcro, the sticky fastening used on clothes and shoes. Burdock, a kind of thistle, grows its seeds in a fruit called a burr, which is covered in tiny hooks. The hooks stick to the fur of passing animals, which help to disperse the seeds. The inventor of Velcro copied this idea. He covered one nylon strip with tiny hooks and another with tiny loops. The two strips stick when they are pressed together, but can easily be pulled apart.

Get this!

People once used hollow grasses to suck up their drinks. This was how drinking straws were invented.

A sticky trap

The sundew plant is a carnivorous plant, which catches insects and feeds on them. The leaves are covered with tiny hairs coated with droplets of glue. The glue looks like sweet nectar, attracting flies which stick to the leaves and are unable to escape. This plant inspired the invention of the fly-trap, a safe and easy way to kill flies. The trap is a strip of yellow plastic – a bright colour known to attract flies – that is coated with a layer of glue.

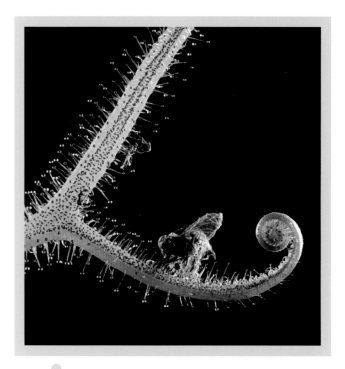

The leaves of the giant water lily inspired the design of the Crystal Palace. The building, like the leaves, was held up by a network of supporting ribs.

The sundew plant traps flies with its sticky glue. The same idea was used to create sticky fly-traps.

A new kind of building

About 150 years ago, an enormous building was built in London. Made entirely from iron and glass, it was known as the Crystal Palace. How could such a huge building be so light and yet so strong? The answer lay in a plant. The leaves of the giant water lily are light enough to float, yet strong enough to carry a child. This is because, on the underside, there is a network of criss-crossing ribs. The designer, Joseph Paxton, had noticed this, and used similar ribs, made from iron, in the Crystal Palace.

Conserving plants

Plants provide us with food, oxygen and many other things, yet we dig them up, cut them down, and poison them with chemicals. It is vital that we care for plants and conserve them for the future.

Plants under pressure

All over the world, plants are being destroyed. As the human population grows, more land is cleared for building and farming. At the same time, industry causes more air pollution which is also harmful for plants. Scientists fear that one-quarter of all plant species could become extinct in the next 50 years. Plants have many useful properties, many of which are still unknown. If we allow species to disappear, we will lose any future benefits these plants might provide.

Try this!

Count the number of plant species that grow around your school. Can you suggest places where you could grow some more?

In Malaysia and other tropical regions, huge areas of rainforest are being cut down and burned to clear the land for farming.

Cutting down forests

Plants affect the environment in important ways, and destroying them has serious consequences. For example, trees hold the soil together, and soak up huge amounts of rainwater. If forests are cut down – and about half of the Earth's forests have already been destroyed – rainwater simply runs away, causing heavy flooding and washing away the soil. This results in spoilt land where nothing at all can grow. Plants also absorb carbon dioxide. When forests are cut down, the level of carbon dioxide in the air increases, causing global warming.

Plant scientists, known as botanists, travel around the world, looking for new plant species.

Get this!

In 2004, one of the world's most important prizes – the Nobel Peace Prize – was awarded to a Kenyan woman called Wangari Maathi. Maathi founded an organisation which has planted over 30 million trees.

Conserving plants

Many people are working to conserve plants. Scientists and conservationists are working with governments to restore natural plant habitats. They have set up national parks, nature reserves and other protected areas. They also travel to every corner of the world to find new plants, investigate them and collect their seeds. In this way, plants that are threatened with extinction can be reintroduced to the wild.

Glossary

Carbohydrates
A group of chemicals that are found in starchy or sugary foods, such as wheat and potatoes. They are also produced during the process of photosynthesis.

Carbon dioxide
One of the gases in air. Plants take in carbon dioxide during photosynthesis.

Conifers
Mostly evergreen trees that grow cones and usually have needle-shaped leaves.

Evolve
To change naturally over time.

Fertiliser
A substance that is added to the soil to provide nutrients for plants to grow.

Fossil fuel
A fuel, such as coal, gas or oil, which formed over millions of years from the remains of animals and plants.

Global warming
The slow warming of the Earth caused by a build-up of carbon dioxide.

Insulator
A material that prevents heat and sound from moving from one place to another.

Nectar
A sugary liquid that is produced by plants to attract insects.

Nutrient
Any substance in the food we eat that gives the body energy or helps it to grow. Also, substances in soil such as potassium and nitrogen, that plants need to grow.

Oxygen
A gas that is found in air and which all animals, including humans, need to survive. All plants give out oxygen during photosynthesis.

Photosynthesis
The process by which plants use the energy in sunlight to turn water from the soil and carbon dioxide from the air into carbohydrates, their food.

Pollution
The harmful substances that spoil the environment.

Protein
A complicated chemical that helps the body to grow and repair itself. Proteins are found in plant foods, such as peas, beans and lentils, as well as in animal foods such as fish, meat and eggs.

Remedy

A treatment that helps to cure a disease or complaint.

Species

A group of the same kind of plant. The oak is a species of tree, for example. Holly, yew and beech are also trees, but each one is a different species.

Spice

A strong-smelling seasoning made from plants and used to flavour food.

Textile

A kind of cloth or fabric.

Websites

www.bbc.co.ukschools/revisewise/ science/living/06_act.shtml
This interactive website looks at the different parts of plants.

www.naturegrid.org.uk/plant/ index.html
Log on to this website to find out more about how people use plants.

www.lanakids.com/plants.html
Find out more about poisonous plants and how to avoid them.

Answers to "What's this?"

Page 11
Wheat

Page 14
Cork oak

Page 16
Oak tree

Page 20
Lavender

Page 23
Potato

Index